Plant Your Dollars in Real Estate and Watch Them Grow

Profit Idea$

Published by

George Sterne
Profit Ideas
8361 Vickers St.
Suite 304
San Diego, CA 92111

ACKNOWLEDGEMENTS

The publishers wish to express thanks to Gene Edelbrock for his contribution of research and writing to this book.

THE MONEY BOOKS

1. Plant your dollars in Real Estate and Watch them Grow.

2. How to make money in the Stock Market

3. Secrets of the Millionaires - How the Rich Made it Big.

4. The Pocket Book of Personal Money Management

5. Secrets of Banking and Borrowing

6. How to start making money in a business of your own.

7. How to Save on Taxes - and take all the deductions you're entitled to.

Preface

If we were to start a garden and knew there was a way we could grow a money tree by following an exact course, don't you think we'd find the way to do this? We would find the time, the place and the means to do it.

Would we learn to fertilize properly giving enough but not too much? Would we carefully select the best place to plant? Would we learn how to prune a tree to get better growth and yield? What about grafting to increase crop production?

If one bothers to do all of these things to harvest a beautiful garden, why not do the same for the cultivation of a real estate empire. Your real estate is like a money tree. All the points about water, fertilizer, grafting and many other things have corresponding match-ups in real estate, as you will see.

You say that you must have the seed to get started? Well, OK, you have the seed right here!

Plant Your Dollars in Real Estate and Watch Them Grow

Contents

Preface

Section I

WHAT'S REAL ESTATE CULTIVATION ALL ABOUT?

Do you have a market for your product?
(— "for a money tree — are you kidding?)

Chapter 1

THE CASE FOR REAL ESTATE

"...Every person who invests in well-selected real estate in a growing section of a prosperous community adopts the surest and safest method of becoming independent, for real estate is the basis of wealth..."

Theodore Roosevelt

"Buying real estate is not only the best way, the quickest way, and the safest way, but the only way to become wealthy..."

Marshall Field

"...Ninety percent of all millionaires become so through owning real estate. More money has been made in real estate than in all industrial investments combined. The wise young man or wage earner of today invests his money in real estate..."

Andrew Carnegie

In studies of the ultra wealthy it has become evident that they didn't earn all that money - few have. The wealth has come from investing money. Almost all the new millionaires, and there are many, have done it by investing it and sheltering it in real estate. Their money works for them and grows.

The ominous inflation we have been seeing has been eroding our buying power. The average wage earner is finding that he can't buy as much as he used to and that his budget keeps getting tighter and tighter. He is having trouble just maintaining his usual life style, much less save anything. How then can we become millionaires? We could invest in the stock market. However, statistics show that only about 2% come away winners*. That is slightly better than Las Vegas. Any earnings are immediately taxable (except when you have some offsetting losses). Let's not count on the stock market.

Tax sheltered annuities and savings programs like IRA and Keogh are good. They definitely build up and you get a good tax advantage from them. The finer programs are generally offered by the better insurance companies. Life insurance is also a good way of saving. Why can these companies offer their subscribers a 2.5% - 3% compounding on their deposits? Simple answer - BECAUSE THEY INVEST IN REAL ESTATE. Who are the richest corporations around? The insurance companies, because they own so much land! How do they do it? They use **Other People's Money** - (their policy holders) to buy land.

How good an investment is putting money in a bank or savings and loan? If you are living in a state of inflation of at least 6% and they are paying you less than that in interest, you are already losing money. The interest they pay you is also taxable, so you are losing more than you think. What are they doing with your money anyway? You guessed it. As much as their government charter will allow, they are sinking it into real estate. There obviously is a better way to invest than leaving our money in a bank or savings and loan.

What makes income property such a good investment?

There are several advantages that real estate offers that other forms of investment can't offer:

1.   It is a hedge against inflation - as things become more

*1.   Jefferson Standard
*2.   McClean, P.2

3

costly, so does your property - many times it is faster than the inflation itself;

2. You get a tax write-off and pay less income tax even though you may take in more money than you are spending on your property;

3. You can finance most of your wealth with Other People's Money;

4. The property, if structured properly, pays for itself as it goes along;

5. Your tenants, by making your principle payments, are actually financing your wealth.

Then, if millionaires make it in real estate, and savings and loan companies make it in real estate, and if insurance companies get rich in real estate why should we invest with them? Why don't **we** invest in real estate?

NOTES

Chapter Two

THE REAL ESTATE MARKET - IT'S HERE TO STAY

Can you picture taxes going down? How soon do you expect the cost of labor to go down? You probably have the same feeling for building costs. The whole world is in an upward inflationary spiral. The government is paying previous debts with inflated dollars. The government cannot let go of the tiger's tail. We are all paving the way with inflated money. There are few things that can act as a hedge against inflation. Some of these things can even make money for you as you go along. Regardless of what they are, they cannot do for you what real estate can do. Real estate can be bought without risk, with leverage, used as collateral, doesn't take an educated eye (as would gems and antiques), cannot be stolen, can be financed, traded, can be rented so that it pays its own way and reduce the amount of income taxes you pay.

By the law of supply and demand, real estate has to be worth more in the future than it is now. There is **not** unlimited land. Many cities have already reached their saturation point in water and sewer supply, in addition to overtaxed electric and gas supply. We have already foreseen that the costs will only make the cost of building new projects go up. This automatically makes the existing property values rise.

Right now you could throw a dart at a map of the United States and make money buying the property you hit - some better than others, but it all rises commensurately.

There are many areas that are sure bets, but we are calculating in truth, reality and real estate.

Another reality is that the country (the world) has been in an inflation rate of at least 6 percent for years, whereas the rate of appreciation of real estate has been consistantly substantially higher than that rate. In Southern California the rate of inflation (or appreciation) the last few years has been close to double that of the national inflation rate. Can you see why this makes such a wonderful hedge for your invested dollar?

NOTES

8

Section II

How To Plant Your
Real Estate Tree

*Most gardens are judged by their beauty. Is a grove? No,
it is judged by how much it produces. Would you suffer to
have an ugly, stinky, noisy oil well in your backyard? (Undoubtedly you wouldn't have to suffer with it for long.)
Let's develop the perspective that it's not our property, it's
our bank statement.*

Chapter Three

CAN'T TELL YOUR GARDEN WITHOUT A PLACARD

To make your money tree grow, study your gardening basics. In order to safeguard your plant you need to understand concepts of irrigation, soil content, fertilizer and sun intensity. Similarly, you need to understand a few concepts about real estate investment.

What Makes it Grow? - Appreciation

For years we have been living in a sustained period of inflation (at least 6%). For example, if you take a home of $50,000 appreciating (inflating) at 6% it would be

$$50,000 \times .06 = 3,000$$

After one year, the property would be worth

$$50,000 + 3,000 = \textbf{53,000}$$

Appreciation through inflation is a key factor in what we're proposing.

To cite an example of another form of appreciation, let's look at a family with 4 kids and 4 dogs buying a home at the end of the street. Shortly after they are in, the street is continued, bringing in a shopping center several blocks down, and then continuing on giving freeway access.

The property automatically becomes more desireable (appreciation) even though the kids are detrimental to the house, and the dogs wrecking the yard (depreciation).

How Much Fertilizer? - Leverage

Our plan is predicated upon the concept that the more property you control in your name, the more appreciation you will have. For illustrative purpose let's take 3 sets of investors with $50,000 to invest. We will assume an inflation rate of 6%.

The **1st Investor** plunks all his $50,000 in a house and owes nothing (100%).

The **2nd Investor** puts his $50,000 down and owes $50,000 against a $100,000 house (50% equity).

The **3rd Investor** wrangles a deal to put his $50,000 against some apartments worth $500,000 (10% equity).

Investor #1	Investor #2	Investor #3
50,000 home	100,000 home	500,000 apartments

Investor #1	Investor #2	Investor #3
50,000 home	100,000 home	500,000 apartments
3,000 6% appreciation	**6,000** 6% appreciation	**30,000** 6% appreciation
53,000 value in 1 year	106,000 value in 1 year	530,000 value in 1 year
3,000 divided by 50,000 is	6,000 divided by 50,000 is	30,000 divided by 50,000 is
6% gain on 50,000 investment in 1 year	12% gain on 50,000 investment in 1 year	60% gain in 1 year

Are the Roots Down There? - Equity

If you own a $50,000 home, and you owe $40,000 against it, your equity is $10,000.

$$\$50,000 - \$40,000 = \$10,000$$

As payments are made and monthly deposits are paid toward the principle, your equity increases. Also, as demonstrated above, as the property appreciates your equity increases. This is one of the main objectives of our investment program. It is also axiomatic that the more property you hold (by using leverage) the more your equity grows through appreciation or inflation.

Does It Need That Much Water? - Depreciation

As long as we're in this rental business, the government gives us a good assist. They know our buildings won't last and that eventually we'll have to replace them. They will permit us to defray that depreciation over a number of

11

years. We can deduct this as an expense to the business. If we have a $50,000 building on a $20,000 lot, we can charge off that $50,000. (the $20,000 on land theoretically never wears out.) If we were to elect to charge off this $50,000 evenly over 25 years*, we could include $2,000 annual expense to **depreciation.** This is what makes income property so lucrative. Although the apartments may be bringing in more money than we are spending, through the inclusion of depreciation, **on paper** it looks as if we are losing money. This loss on rental property can be subtracted from our earned income (salaries, etc.) We pay less tax because we netted less. This is called our **tax shelter.** At this point, let it suffice that we may not want to lean too heavily on depreciation at the beginning of our program. The government aims to get it back sooner or later.

Can We Graft on Another Producing Branch?
"New Starter"

After you get your tree bearing, you may be able to improve your yield by grafting on another bloomer. Your main plant could be embellished upon by including with it a new plant or piece of property. Anytime you can pick up a bargain, you could include it with your main package when selling or trading to increase your equity and depreciation. This will also shorten the time interval needed between your main property transactions.

Now we have the basics for our garden. Through keep-

---

*There are several popular forms of depreciation for different purposes. The mose basic as illustrated above is called **Straight line.**

See Appendix E for different kinds of depreciation. Appendix F for their application.

ing our **equity** low, we use **leverage** for **appreciation and depreciation.** We will service our tree around these concepts. If we have a 10% equity, 90% of our crop is done with **O**ther **P**eople's **M**oney - welcome to the **OPM** Club. If forces other than your own capital can make you money, why not join their team - or better yet, have them join your team.

NOTES

14

Section III

How to Plant Your Money Producer for Sturdy Growth

Monopoly

Most of us at one time or another have played the game "Monopoly". There are some valuable lessons to be learned even though it is only a game - the person with no property is at the mercy of those who have it. The rich get richer, the poor get poorer.

In the game, it is a matter of chance as to who gets the right properties first. In real life we need not wait - we should determine our course of action and then do it.

Chapter Four

LET'S START DIGGING!

Do you have life insurance? If you have a whole life policy (not term), you have paid in some cash that has been accruing interest. (The insurance company has been investing in real estate, remember?). They will be glad to lend you these cash values. Sounds great? The best is yet to come. The rate at which they lend this is between 4% and 6%! There are few bargains like this around anywhere Certainly you are going to make more than 6% on your real estate investment. (Remember, the chart on page 7 of three investors?)

So you don't have an insurance policy. How about your dad or father-in-law? They would have much more in it available to borrow. If you borrowed say 10,000 of his money, you could offer him a 2nd trust deed held on your new investment and pay him back with higher interest. His insurance money is secured, he is making more on it than if it stayed in his account, and you are on your way.

If you have an equity in your home, you can start here. Go to your lender and ask him to increase your loan to the maximum. It will raise your payments, and interest rate, but it will be worth it when you put it to work...

If you can build up an equity in income property to three times the amount of the value of that home you have, you probably wouldn't be satisfied with that house any longer anyway.

Why be happy with a castle (your home paid for or not), when there's a **kingdom** at your grasp? If a few years by staying within your plan, you would have the purchasing power to pay cash for that home, if you were so foolish to so elect.

Income property is such a good deal that many people are buying new homes for 10% - 15% down and then renting them out. In anticipation of the great appreciation they will get, they think nothing of renting these houses for several hundred dollars less than the payments (an example of **negative cash flow).**

Would you not be better off to sell your house to invest in real estate, and then rent one of these new homes yourself?

You don't own your home? How about your dad, father-in-law? Again, offer him the security of that second trust deed - he will probably be glad to help you. You **could** offer him a partnership and buy him out later (although I'd prefer other routes first).

Are you a veteran? There are some fabulous opportunities for vets to buy with little down. If you can capitalize on this, it will get you started. You can trade this house later on.

Do you own your car? Is it worth a year or two driving a cheaper car to send you on the road to success? Remember our dedication to the money tree? If you have an equity in a good car, sell it and drive a less expensive model for a short time.

In the next chapter we will show you that the more money you can start with, the better off you are. How about using several of these above sources of money - it will all come back soon, greatly multiplied.

If you have no credit anywhere, there are still ways to get into real estate.

In some cases a seller will be interested in leasing the property to you and giving you the option of buying it at or before the end of the term (lease option). A contract of this type can be as flexible as you two want to make it. Many times the lease rent is applied as a down payment, but not necessarily. It is a good way for the intended buyer to take a piece of property off the market for a year or so. If the property appreciates higher than anticipated, the person leasing has made some money. Ordinarily, to compensate the seller for this risk, the price is jacked up. Again, it is a contract written between two people. How good a bargainer are you?

A statement should certainly be included in the lease giving you the right at any time to sell your option or the property. If you don't sell you must eventually qualify to assume the existing loan or create a new one.

For someone who has no present money or good credit, he can still tie up a piece of property and enjoy the benefits of it. This vehicle has several names, but is primarily known as the **land contract.** The potential seller keeps title in his name and the buyer makes payments as contracted. Everything is OK as long as the buyer keeps honoring his contract. If he defaults, he is not offered the protection of a default in trust deeds. However, the payments are still being made in the name of the seller. The lending institution does not have the right to refuse such a transaction.

This situation can linger on until the buyer can get OK'd by the lender - or until he has a good sized equity in property and/or he can get it refinanced elsewhere, or sold.

Warning - if the seller is unethical, he can sometimes take advantage of you - title transfer cannot always be assured. This route should bear the scrutiny of your attorney

If we still haven't succeeded in getting you into your first property let's try another way. Ghetto property is always turning over and you can get into it more cheaply than other property. If you haven't been able to get started with any of the aforementioned methods, you need help. Swallow a little pride and buckle up for a year. I'll bet there are VA or FHA foreclosures down in that ghetto or fringe area that you can get into for a song. -It would oblige you to live there for a short time (at least legally), but then you're free to sell or exchange. In chapter 8 there are some suggestions on how to pick up some of this property for littleor nothing - you're at the point where you have little to lose except the difficult position you're in.

There is still another way if you can afford to invest a certain amount of cash per month. You would need to join hands with several others in a group investment. To do this you would need to find a real estate syndicator who specialized in group investment. An imaginative syndicator can be a magician if you can find him.

It is not so important which technique or approach you use. What is important is that you do something and get underway and with as much equity as you can possibly conjure up. All of the ways are good - but it is important to get started under intelligent and well thought out guidelines.

NOTES

Chapter Five

BUY IT RIGHT!

Your goal is to mushroom your equity into as great an amount as possible. It becomes academic that if you are compounding your equity at each turnover, it is especially important to put as much money to work as possible.

To prove this point, let us use the following chart as a demonstration. We are going to double some numbers ten times.

1	2	3	4	5	6	7	8	9	10
1	2	4	8	16	32	64	128	256	512
3	6	12	24	48	96	192	384	768	1536
4	8	16	32	64	128	256	512	1024	2048

After 10 steps 1 has progressed to 512
3 compounds to 1536
4 compounds to 2048

As illustrated in the chart, if you start out with 3 times as much, you will end up with three times as much (3x512= 1536).

If you start out with 4 times as much you will end up with four times as much. (4 x 512 = 2048).

By pyramiding you are anticipating a series of sales and/or exchanges. In each move you hope to double the value of what you are going into. You may not always achieve this, nor is it necessarily your game plan, but it is something hoped for and often is achievable.

We have illustrated in our chart that by doubling the number four ten times, we'd end up with a total of 2,048. If we were talking about starting our investment with an equity of $4,000 and doubled it 10 times we would pyramid this figure to $2,048,000. Maintaining an equity of

10%, we would have compounded that $4,000 cash to a net worth of $204,800.

It's time to get started and to **buy it right.**

NOTES

NOTES

Chapter Six

PRINCIPLES OF PYRAMIDING

There are two main concepts that are of paramount importance, 1. to get started; and
2. to start with as much equity and leverage as possible.
Let's take a hypothetical trip through a few progressions to show what can be done*.

Step One

For example let's start with a single family dwelling in an unattractive part of town. It may have been foreclosure you probably offered the party a few hundred dollars to sign off his interest (via a quit claim deed) shortly before his 90 days were up. (This procedure will be explained in Chapter 8). You undoubtedly have 3-6 months of payments to make up but you're still in for a song.

Spend some time cleaning the place and doing some simple cosmetics - paint, repair, perhaps a cement walk to the steps or door - anything to make the place look better without really spending money.

It is worth some time to visit tract homes. The models

---

*There have been many books written on pyramiding. Two in particular are good and go into detail on buying bargain properties. Nickerson is the patriarch of them all and Haroldson is excellent and elaborates more on financing and refinancing properties. Both should be read, but keeping in mind that they (especially Nickerson) were written some time ago and that many figures just don't hold true anymore and certainly IRS regulations have changed in reference to depreciation and exchanging properties.

are professionally done and you can pick up some wonderful ideas that are inexpensive. One such is the use of hanging plants and greenery (either simulated or real) and wall paper or bright colors. These pros understand the psychology of making things feel homey. It costs you little to copy their professional techniques. These ideas can sell and rent your properties.

Now rent this house to someone that will look good on paper. You want top rental money because that makes your property worth more. If you can put somebody in there that will pay like clockwork, you have some saleable merchandise. The government is a good tenant. Let's rent it to a welfare tenant and have her **request** that her rent be sent directly to you.

Now you immediately have something ready to turn over to Step #2.

After acquiring this first property, you also could pick up something similar to this and put them together to boost your equity toward Step 2. This is what I referred to as "grafting".

Anytime you can pick up an additional cheapy, by all means do it. I assure you that by such a practice you will be well on your way to compounding your equity. (At this time, it is debatable as to whether you trade your property or sell. This is the point where I was referring to pruning - we want to look down the road a bit and to get the greatest possible yield we can. More on this in the Appendix E and Chapter 7).

Capitalization

Sound logic tells us that the greater the profit, the higher the market will bring. This is mostly how income property values are calculated. There are formulas predicated upon monthly or annual income - both gross income (without

26

taking out any expenses) and net income (after deducting expenses). It still comes to the reality that the greater the income, the higher the value of the property.

A prospective buyer is not going to see how much money you took in. He is buying future rent based on the **present rents,** and your history of vacancies and other expenses. Create a chart showing the days your units were filled. It matters not, if the tenants were in there for 1/2 rent or whatever. You are creating a realistic image for vacancy factor. Through capitalization formulas, if you can prove your vacancy factor is low, you can legitimately get more when you sell. (See Appendix B)

Step Two

That worked so beautifully, let's try it again. We want about 3-4 units. That same part of town is good enough for us. There are apartments available down there through foreclosure - we could perhaps try that one again. We could be looking for this deal while we're still working on Step 1. Tenants in this part of town can be less than ideal, therefore some owners are motivated to get out - this works to your advantage. As long as we have equity, we could perhaps use a broker in the area.

We hope to get into these 3-4 units, cosmetize them, and again put in our clockwork welfare tenants and sell quickly while it physically looks good, and before the tenants want to move. (Just because their payments are being mailed, doesn't make them less fickle. It just looks good on paper to your new buyer).

By this time we're really on our way.

At this point we will graduate into something bigger **when** we can find something that will carry its own weight without risking everything.

We may have to wait awhile for appreciation to increase

our equity.

We could refinance these apartments, and pull out some money to start again with another such "starter" house or perhaps another 3-4 units. If we did, we could possibly lessen the time necessary for our next step.

Step Three

We should be into 8-12 units and we can have units anywhere. Please remember, it is what comes out on paper that is important to you. This is the step that can best be made in buying a run-down apartment from a motivated seller. It is absolutely amazing what paint, carpeting and drapes can do to completely change the appearance of a place. If necessary, borrow a little to purchase carpets and drapes. You could perhaps borrow on your building from the lender (or lenders), but now you are a busines person with a sizeable equity. If you have money, you can borrow from a bank. It makes it easier for the next time you need to borrow, so let's establish some credit at your bank.

If you remember the capitalization factor it's important for the market value of your apartments to bring in top rent and have no vacancies. When trying to sell or exchange, be sure to have every unit filled, even if you have to move someone in for a first month free. If that apartment is filled, you count that person as paying.

By now you should be enjoying the advantages of being a landlord. You are not giving as much to the government, you have more to spend, life should be more enjoyable because you **know** where you are going and it is reassuring - it's fun!

It is suggested that by this time you should have acquired a capable, responsible realtor that is sophisticated in tax situations and perhaps some syndication. He will be able to pay his way with you in what he can save you in eventual taxes and in determining what and when to buy.

At this point there are many tempting variations you can attack, but it is strongly advised that you stay in your game plan of residential income property.

Step Four

You should be able to move into 16-24 units. It could perhaps be time for a manager. Your properties and equities should financially be able to take care of themselves with reasonable supervision from you.*

You are working with time, and patience is needed until you can work up your equity. You can do nothing about increasing the inflation factor (leave that to the President!), but you **can** keep your property in good condition physically and from the point of profit - remember what capitalization does?

If you had some equity in some other property to add to your 16-24 units, you could cut down this interim wait that you're enduring, waiting for your accruing equity to carry into step 5.

Don't forget that anywhere along the way you can start another sequence - perhaps you don't care to start again in the risky part of town, but there are other opportunities to pick up some bargains. Remember now, you have a financial statement and credit established at your bank. You can borrow money any time you find a bargain to buy.

I'd rather not elaborate past step 5. You should be into 30-50 units or possibly into another equally advantageous forms of income property. By the time you're at step 3, I assume you'll be sophisticated enough to know what is going on. You don't even have to be smart, just smart enough to find the right realtor you can trust and who'll take care of you the rest of the way up (it's good for him, too). You two will end up good friends because of the mutually good thing you're doing for each other.

*The procedure of buying run down apartments and inexpensively fixing them up will almost always pay you dividends.

**Remember the compounding theory of pyramiding money. One good rule is never to pull out money from equity unless it is to reinvest - live on your earned income or salary.

NOTES

Section IV

How to Pluck Your Dollars Right From the Money Tree

AUCTION ACTION!

Kids sometime start the prank of looking and pointing up into the sky. Soon everyone is looking up. There are several variations, but basically, it tells of crowd psychology.

Merchandise in a retail store could sit for a long time with no action. However, the same merchandise at the same price during a mammoth sale goes quickly. This behavior is evident in auctions.

I have witnessed auctions at van and storage warehouses when unclaimed boxes were sold for overdue storage fees. It can really be wild to see the exorbitant prices people bid for a box of which nobody knows the contents. If action is there, people are drawn into it. Conversely, even if the property is valuable, if nobody shows interest, others are reluctant to join in. Odd, perhaps, but this is what happens and some real values slip through.

Chapter Seven

EXCHANGE VERSUS SELL

When you **sell** your income property for a profit, and it records in the county recorder's office, you owe the government money - even if you take your proceeds and invest them that very same day into some other income property.

If you haven't held the property longer than 12 months*, IRS figures that any profit is included as personal income and is taxed as such. If it has been held beyond that point, you pay tax only on half of that **capital gain.**

If that property is exchanged, then it is not currently taxed - it is not tax free, because the government anticipates they'll get their hands on it sooner or later. Let's call an exchange **tax deferred,** not tax exempt. (When the government succeeds it is called **recovery**).

In an exchange situation, whenever any cash is brought out of the transaction and not reinvested, it is called **boot** and is taxable.

Let us remember what our goal is - we are not primarily aiming at sheltering our income, we are trying to build a large estate. If we take too much depreciation at the early stages, it could effect the shelter when we need it more later on. (For further explanation, see Appendix E on depreciation).

To avoid becoming too complicated, let's just say at this time, it is to our advantage for our purpose of estate build-

---

*The number of months required for capital gains changes from time to time as tax laws are revised.

ing to take just enough depreciation to keep from making a profit on paper.

In some older real estate investment books you will find expressions like free exchange. Don't fault the author, tax regulations change and they will change some more. Free advice from the wrong person is no bargain. A fee paid to a tax accountant or attorney is a good investment - get up to date.

NOTES

35

Chapter Eight

SOME BARGAINS

As long as this country has a free enterprise system, some people will experience financial problems. Through a series of combinations of many things that can happen, people end up in a financial crisis.

Through absolutely no fault of their own, responsible, capable, honest, high-calibre people end up in a financial crisis. A series of combinations of many things can happen. A person could have an illness or injury, or a family death or divorce could happen. Perhaps that person affected could be an employer and he goes bankrupt, thereby pulling some unsuspecting, undeserving person under. A lost government contract or an industry shutting down can chain react in the lives of many secondary families. Weather can effect business: too much rain, not enough rain, too much snow, wind, sun. Unavoidable things can effect our lives financially. For one reason or another people can no longer afford to make payments on their homes and/or need their equity out of them.

When a party falls behind on payment, the creditor (trust deed holder) protects himself by **foreclosure.** He serves legal notice of his intention by filing a **"notice of default"**. The delinquent party then has 90 days to bring his account current before things get worse. Your county recorder's office lists these notices of default, and you can bet there will be more than a few opportunists out attempting to buy up the distressed party's equity (at a fat discount, of course).

Toward the end of the 90 day period, the delinquent is generally not in a very good position to bargain. He must

36

catch up the whole delinquent amount (including charges and penalties). If he doesn't, he has only 21 days left before he is completely stripped of all interest in the property. In these last 21 days, he must pay off the entire amount of the account **in full** plus penalties and charges. If this isn't taken care of, the property goes to auction (called the trustee sale).

When this trustee sale goes to auction, the trust deed holder has the option to bid the entire amount owed him on paper, and from that point or amount, the auction ensues. Incredibly, sometimes nobody even shows up. Of course, the better the property and the greater the equity, the more activity there is in attendance and bidding.* The sequence of foreclosure is outlined in Appendix G.

At these sales only cash or certified checks are acceptable.

Again, anytime up to that 90 day point, the delinquent party can sell his interest, and the prospective buyer would have to bring the account up to date.

Caution - anyone in this much trouble generally has other things that have also slid - he held onto his house tenaciously - other creditors may have successfully sued and put a lien on the house. If that is the case, that lien would have to be satisfied before title could come into the buyer's name.

There are several other different means by which property can hit the auction block. Auctions can be exciting and the unbelievable is commonplace. Worthless properties are sold for unwarranted high prices - some type of hysteria seems to overtake some people. Sometimes, for

---

*Let us assume you have become the successful bidder. You leave a deposit of 10% and generally have 30 days to raise the balance. Most other types of auctions require cash or certified funds for the entire amount. There are many variations of this format.

unknown reason valuable property draws little interest and goes for pennies on the dollar.

The investor who is diligent, does his research and is prepared (cash, in most cases) will eventually come up with a good buy - especially if he is willing to check into the less glamorous areas.

Some other types of auctions:

Sheriff's sale - when a creditor has taken a debtor to court and has been awarded a judgment, the amount becomes a lien against the property and can actually in some cases, cause the property to be sold at auction. These sales are supposed to be advertised and posted both on the property and in the courthouse.

Some fantastic stories occasionally are heard where $25,000 properties are picked up for car repair bills of a few hundred dollars. Can you spare the time to familarize yourself with the courthouse posters and such sales?

Tax sale - When the property taxes go unpaid, the property is deeded to the state. The owner can redeem this anytime within a 5 year period by paying the back taxes and a slight penalty. However, after that 5 year period, the property is **eligible** to be sold for taxes. That doesn't automatically mean it will be.

There are many properties in the back country which have been long forgotten, with taxes unpaid. Perhaps the owner died and present-ownership is unknown or those inheriting the property cannot be reached through lost or inadequate addresses. After the five year period, if some citizen requests that this go to auction, then the property will be brought out to the auction block.

Sometimes these property sites are difficult to find and people don't bother to drive around the back country to locate them. These properties can often be picked up for back taxes. These are excellent "starters" or "new starters" as property held with nothing owing gives you great leverage for exchanging.

Do you have time to check with your local tax collector's office for details?

Trustee sales - These have already been covered to some extent. These sales must be advertised in the local paper of circulation (sometimes just the local newspaper, sometimes a city has a "trade" newspaper which post such sales, notices of fictitious names and the legal notices required by law). People have been competing for 90 days and 21 days for these bargains.

The old pros don't bother with such properties unless there is a husky balance left in it for them. There is still a good margin for your starter. The lesser bargains will still be there - especially if you are willing to go into a riskier part of town.

Administrator sales - When a widow, widower or single person dies without a will (intestate), if there are no survivors (and sometimes when so elected by the survivors), the county is appointed **administrator** to settle the estate and to pay taxes. Your county holds such a sale. This is done periodically where a public auction is held. These attract a lively gathering. The prime properties naturally get an enthused reaction and bidding goes accordingly. However, the lesser properties and the remote properties that are difficult to find, hold some real bargains. The county appraised value is slightly lower than the true market value. The bidder is obliged to start his bidding at 90% of this appraised price. Some bargains will slip through here.

By a phoned request, most county public administrators will put you on their mailing list. (They also auction off vehicles, mobile homes, trailers and many varied personal effects.)

Do you have the time to find out from your county administrator's office what it's procedures are?

The Ensign Pulver Theory

If an off-color story brings across an important real estate theorum, I assume the strategy excuses the means.

In the movie Mr. Roberts, the outlandish character Ensign Pulver was confiding to Doug Roberts how he fell heir to some girl's virginity. It was simple, he said, nobody before had ever asked her!

I don't necessarily recommend this in social life, but this principle applied to real estate is beautiful. It costs you absolutely nothing to offer - (not even a slap in the face)!

Sooner or later you will fall heir to a real winner. Let's make a few offers!

Chapter 9

SOME MORE BARGAINS

Out of Town Ownership

Many times unused property is owned by people out of town. Perhaps they inherited it or had to leave town never to come back. Maybe it is owned by some old folks who will never make use of it. Quite a bit of unused back country property is owned by someone who lives elsewhere . This can also apply to city lots that are unused. This is the perfect time to use your Ensign Pulver Technique - it costs you nothing to make an offer, and if you make enough offers. one will eventually drop into your hands.

The county recorder's office can be a valuable tool in your hands. The office is required to keep records that can be of great assistance to you:

1. names alphabetically of all property owners and the addresses to where the tax bills are sent;

2. property listed by parcel, book and lot number. This also tells you who the owner is and mailing address. It also breaks down that property description to street address (if in the city). Conversely, the street addresses are cross indexed so you can pick up owners by either address or lot number;

3. The date the property transaction last took place.

Executor sales

When an attorney is handling the estate of a deceased client, the property frequently has to be sold to pay taxes and costs (including the attorney's). Any money left over is to be distributed through inheritance distribution. Many different styles are used here - some explicitly legitimate and some rather obscure. However, someone is getting to them - can you?

Trust sales

This is the same operation as an attorney acting as an executor, the difference being that this executor power has been left to an instituton - generally a bank. Most banks have a trust department (even if only in the main branch). A routine tour of these officials and getting to know them can pay dividends. Who is the trust officer in your bank?

Divorce

Heavy divorce loads in recent years have somewhat altered the procedures. With equal rights and with divorce up, the judges are obliged to point for speedy action and liquid settlements. In the absence of a pre-hearing settlement, the judge more frequently says "sell" and split the leftovers. (In equal rights the man has his rights to community property, too.)

Naturally all the realtors are aware of this too and they are out to compete for the listing as soon as the divorce hits the paper. (This is true also for the death list). However, the realtors rarely follow this up properly. About 45 days **after** they filed for divorce, the couple has had its day before the judge - **then** is the time to approach them. The judge has pushed them closer to the sale. Here is another good place for Ensign Pulver Technique.

FHA and VA Resales

The government occasionally forecloses on houses. They bring them up to high quality condition and then turn around and sell them. (The government takes a licking on this phase, but it's a good deal for the purchaser).

If you qualify by making enough money to fit their formula, you can get into these for extremely low down payment. You are obliged to live in them for a period (subject to change but currently 6 months), but then you're legitimately entitled to sell. Here is another starter. Check the want ads. Some broker is specializing in selling these properties.

NOTES

Section V

Does this Gardener Have Patience?

In 1923 Germany had a spectacular inflationary bust. In order to buy groceries people literally carried their paper money to the market in bushel baskets and wheelbarrows.

I spoke with a German couple who had personally experienced the melee and later came to Southern California where they engaged in Real Estate Purchases.

I asked them who came out best in the rapidly changing times--

1. The person with his home paid off.

2. The person with 50% equity.

3. The highly leverage individual.

The response was immediate and emphatic - the highly leverage person came out best because the balance was paid off with inflated money.

In essence this is what we're experiencing in these times but at a less exaggerated rate. Aren't we trying to pay things off with inflated money?

Chapter Ten

SURVEY OF REAL ESTATE

Let's look at some of the different kinds of real estate in order to select what will be best for you.

Business and Commercial - There is a lot of money to be made in business and commercial property - especially in the development thereof. There is also a lot being lost here. Shopping center developments, economic trends, overloaded areas - there are a good many reasons why any but the experts should steer clear of these investments, and even these get burned.

Farmland - There are some beautiful moves that can be done with groves, especially in Southern California, and Florida, but those are geared more for speculation and tax shelter than building an estate and empire. Somewhere along the line, if you start a second pyramid, you might use that for speculation and perhaps do some good things with it, like buying unimproved land and installing groves. After 2-5 years in this, and subdividing your groves, creating some building sites within a bearing grove, you can do well. There are numerous prosperous such ventures - but that doesn't fit your picture and what you're doing. Remember, you are building an estate.

Raw land - There is money to be made here also. If you depend upon luck, you can sometimes do well. You can get stymied and bogged down with your capital. If you know something that looks like a sure fire return because of a freeway, a shopping center, a manufacturing development - then this can be a windfall, if you know what you're doing.

This type of investment also does not fit your picture,

unless again you have started a new project that you can afford to speculate with.

This type of investment is better suited for the long term investor who can invest his money and be patient until the investment matures.

Leverage is not available, nor is other people's money, nor is depreciation (and taxes do go on).

Some Pitfalls

Resort properties are notorious for attracting people to the "ideal" life. The SBA* knows that these are a shaky risk as so many quirks of fate effect these up and down businesses. Resist the temptation, danger lurks here, and many have ventured into the trap and lost everything.

Many will make money on fads and when overbuilt and over-competitive, or the fad passes, many enterprises will lose. Those investors in residential income property will still be pyramiding. (People will always need residential property).

Fads are dangerous. In the 40's miniature golf was popular, in the 50's it was bowling, in the 60's trampolines, in the 70's racquetball and skateboard parks.

Awkward financing can bog you down. If payments are too big and there are too many trust deed, it can become a

*For the importance of the overall success of the US economy, it is important to keep healthy the small business enterprise segment. The Small Business Administration is the Federal government agency for lending to this smaller but important phase of our economy.

When there are droughts, floods, freezes etc., there is an influx of government money to assist the afflicted. For other legitimate reasons also the money is available. The SBA definitely is well aware of what happens in the resort business.

difficult task to sell the property. If a property cannot be refinanced, many times the anticipated seller will wait a long time before being able to turn it over. For instance, if your property is substandard for some reason, banks and lending institutions will not lend on it. Some examples to watch out for:

- not connected to water sources (other than well);
- not on paved road;
- access to property through easement only;
- functional obsolescense - like not having a forced air

heating system.

The facility of easy financing is most generally the key to selling a property easily.

Residential Income Property

There are many good reasons why you're better off in a residential income property. You have leverage, OPM, depreciation and a guaranteed future market. Let's look at that future market.

The Have-not Vacuum

A situation is being created whereby young people cannot afford to buy a home or even a condominium. They lack the down payment. In the years to come it will require greater and greater capital in order to buy into a property. People without an equity won't be able to crack the nut, because they haven't grown with the inflation/appreciation. A vacuum is being created where those now (or shortly) without property will not be able to own property. They will be renters.

The apartment and condominium situation doesn't

really get better either. Because of building regulations the builders cannot put as many units in the same space as they used to. It is not as profitable for them to build an apartment - the ratio of cost per unit (largely due to land cost) doesn't invite them to build on the smaller lots zoned for multiple residence. It is profitable for them to build high density only. Even as such, the "have-not vacuum" will reach this level also.

There are many cities and county communities that are having growth expanding problems and subsequently throw on a building moratoriam. If the sewer, water, gas and electric supplies are overburdened, we shall see the cities and counties tightening up more and more on multi-family and high density dwellings. What is this going to do to apartments? The most basic rule in economics is based on supply and demand. The more need for a fixed number of apartments makes a greater demand for them - meaning higher prices for apartments. That also means more appreciation. (Of course, there will also be the need for rental homes too.) Let's get started in residential income property.

NOTES

NOTES

51

Chapter Eleven

REALTORS -
HOW TO FIND THE RIGHT ONE

My tax accountant once told me, "If I can't save you the amount I'm asking, don't pay me". I was always happy to pay his bill.

Let's use this same logic with your real estate broker. You can, through effort, wits and gumption get yourself off the ground and pretty well on the way to your goal. By trying to do everything yourself, you may overlook something early in your venture that will cost you thousands of dollars in the future. The tax laws are changed yearly, with the IRS plugging holes here and there. What some book tells you might have been good advice 10 years ago, maybe 5 years or even last year. You need good advice on current laws.

Would you pay $50 to an accountant for an hour's interview? You should look down the road a little way - a person holding a million or two in real estate could find a $50 consultation fee a fantastic bargain if it could save him tens of thousands of dollars. Get yourself well briefed from some expert professional advice - ask questions and find the alternatives - then ask these questions of your realtor - if he doesn't know all the answers, he's not sophisticated enough for you to place your entire future with. (You say he's your friend? Would you let your friend take out your appendix?)

Some of these probes could go like this -

Do I want to sell or exchange my first step?

My 2nd?

My 3rd?

I have a good equity in the apartment I need to turn over. Should I exchange or should I refinance and keep my apartments and take my money out to reinvest in other apartments?

Do I pay my capital gains now? When is the best time and the best way to pay them. (That'll separate the salesmen from the pros).

Believe it or not, the answers are not always the same. Much depends on your income, tax bracket, age, economic stability, etc.

Frequently, if not all the time, you will be exchanging your properties while climbing the pyramidal ladder. Most of the exchanges, certainly the most imaginative exchanges in a modern city, are done by a handful of realtors. Find out who they are - will they have enough time to handle you with what you have in mind? (I should think so).

The following chapter will be spent on syndication. Your realtor should be skilled with these tools as well as tax knowledge. Every advantage in real estate can be magnified by an imaginative and skilled syndicator. I will draw an analogy between an automobile and a syndicator. It can be a tremendous vehicle in the right hands, but disastrous in the wrong hands.

A syndicator should be proud of his track record on each venture. Ask to see some of these records - ask for references - ask other syndicators.

Like an accountant or other realtors, he should be worth his services. However, unfortunately, some syndicators become vultures and really pick a few carcasses clean. They can lock you in so that they are using your money for their own advantage. Check around.*

*I highly recommend "Principles of Real Estate Syndication"

53

by Samuel Freshman. Anyone who is going to let someone else invest and control his money certainly owes it to himself to be well informed.

NOTES

Chapter Twelve

SYNDICATION

Syndication is the investment mode of the future because it offers advantages for all types of investors - big or little, and because people will have to invest with pooled resources to get into anything. (Remember the "have-not" vacuum?)

Syndicating is the joining together of two or more people for investment purposes. This can involve taking property jointly, all the way to incorporation. The most advantageous vehicle for our purposes is the limited partnership.

A limited partnership is composed of limited partners and general partner(s). Frequently the syndicator is the general partner and assumes responsibility and liability for running the business. He is paid for such operation (generally a percentage of the income). The limited partners contribute money only and are limited in liability to the amount of their investment (hence the name).

The limited partnership is flexible in its structure so as to gear its advantage to the investor. For instance, a young investor has little to put down, but could possibly contribute $50 a month. With ten to twenty such investors it takes little imagination to see what this could do in the way of leverage.

If retired people banded together in an investment, they could put a larger chunk of capital together in order to come up with spendable income.

A skilled syndicator can mold your needs to the investment.

When banding together, people are compounding their purchasing power. If you have $10,000 to invest by yourself, how much of a bargain can you get? Rarely could you pick up something underpriced by more than $5,000. If we banded together 10 people with $10,000 each, we could move in some directions others can't - we could buy some expensive properties at a trustee sale, a default tax sale, bankruptcy sale and so on. One hundred thousand dollars cash available can frequently buy bargains highly underpriced (especially in acreage). Cash talks, and a good realtor/syndicator can do it for your group.

What do you want a limited partnership to do for you? First, let's realize that all the benefits of real estate investment are still at your disposal within a private limited partnership - appreciation, extreme leverage, OPM, and depreciation. If there are ten such limited partners, each gets 1/10th of the tax loss/gain. A corporation has its depreciation taken out for the corporation entity, is taxed and then distributed to you, where it is then taxed again. The two real advantages are that the limited partnership gets better leverage by banding together, and that you are not involved with management problems. The general partner (generally the syndicator) takes on all management (for a fee, of course).

If we were to set up a limited partnership for your ideal situation, we would look for other investors that had similar goals - long term investment and desiring to put no additional cash into it other than the original investment.

It is extremely important to set this group up correctly and to identify possible problems before they become evident. Some of the items you would want qualified:

1. The limited partners have the right to fire the general partner,
2. the limited partners have the right to terminate and liquidate the partnership;
3. to establish the term of the partnership life and renewal

thereof.
4. To insure proper motivation to the syndicator.

It is also wise to create proper incentives to the general partner for him to stick to the game plan. We don't want him more motivated to build than to sell (give him a piece of the profit). A good, sincere general partner should have a monetary investment in this also.

With the right man at the helm, there's no limit to what he can do for the group.

NOTES

Section VI

Are You Sure the Tree's Growing?

Is There Another Money Tree Around Here?

You are expected to pick up a bargain to get underway. After you are underway, it is easier for you to obtain money for some of the bargains. You should continuously be sleuthing around for such bargains. These bargains could be new starters for a whole new pyramid, or be offered with your initial prime project to give you more equity and to hurry along your progress to the next successive step. You could also use this new starter for a speculative venture that you could afford to gamble with. Keep digging.

Chapter Thirteen

CAN YOU AFFORD TO MOVE YOUR MONEY TREE?

Remember the story of the goose and the golden egg and the moral that you don't kill the goose that lays the golden egg? Let's compare that with our money tree.

You have been shown where your most lucrative soil is to plant your money tree. You have been shown how to maximize growth and production through using leverage, appreciation, depreciation. You have even been given an illustration of how to graft additional limbs (new starters) to make your tree bear more. Are you going to take risks to kill your golden goose or your money tree? As long as your plant is successful, don't experiment.

In your quest for an estate, it is easy after gaining success several steps down the road, to venture out and leave your plan. You will have the capacity to buy a ski lodge, a fishing lodge, a nursery store, gift shop, a bar, etc., that has always been your desire. Sad numbers have lost everything because of these temptations to venture into fields that are unsound or in business they know little about. If a plan is successfully working for you why alter it? Don't leave your game plan. After all, which is more important, taking that little ego trip, or making yourself financially secure by creating a wealthy estate. You will have abundance and be able to enjoy almost anything. Stay with the plan. Don't kill your money tree.

Chapter Fourteen

PLAN AHEAD

The story is told about one hundred men, all born at the same time and starting life with equal opportunity. Sixty-five years later, at normal retirement age, thirty-two have died, sixty-three are dependent on social security, welfare, or the generosity of friends and relatives, four are living comfortably on their incomes from savings and investments, and one is wealthy.

In a lifetime we all earn a fortune. Which do you choose for yourself - dependence or comfort? For the security you want, it is essential to plan ahead, to know where you are going and to stick to your plan. The difference between the "have-nots" and the "haves" is that those who "have" have a plan. Many athletes, actors, entertainers have made fabulous sums of money and have still ended up broke - Why? **Because they had no plan!** It is not even necessary to scrimp and be miserly all your life as some profess. It is only necessary to get a proper plan under way. (By following the plan and ideas in this book, there are many different ways for you to get started, some even without sacrifices of any kind).

The important point to understand is that **you** decide that you are doing to do it and then do it. There is absolutely nothing standing between you and financial security except your own procrastination.

NOTES

BIBLIOGRAPHY

Freshman, Samuel K.
   Principles of Real Estate Syndication, Parker & Son, Los
   Angeles, CA

Haroldson, Mark O.
   How to Wake up the Financial Genius Inside You.
   Marko Enterprises, Salt Lake City, Utah

Nickerson, William
   How I turned $1,000 into a Million in Real Estate - in my
   spare time.
   Simon & Schuster, New York, NY

McClean, L.
   McClean's Property Pyramid
   Nides Cini Publications, Los Angeles, CA

McMichael, Stanley L.
   How to Make Money in Real Estate
   Wilshire Book Company, North Hollywood, CA

Nielson, Jens & Jackie
   How to Save or Make Thousands when you buy or sell
   your house.
   Dolphin Books, Doubleday & Co. Inc., Garden City, NY

APPENDIX A

Cash Flow

Cash flow is the amount of cash left over from gross receipts after all cash expenses. Cash expenses do not include depreciation.

For example, if we had an annual gross income (before expenses) of $12,000 and had actual operating expenses (including payments) of $10,000, there would be $2,000 left over. This 2,000 is what we are putting into our pockets before we include depreciation.

Cash flow = Gross income - Expenses (including payments)

$$CF = GI - E$$

APPENDIX B

Vacancy Factor

In figuring a vacancy factor, the lower the rate, the more in your pocket.

Every unit has an occupancy of 365 days. We will prefer to use 365 days rather than 360. If we had 10 days vacancy-

$$\frac{10}{360} = 2.77\% \text{ while } \frac{10}{365} = 2.73\%$$

the vacancy rate would be a fraction of that 365 expressed first as a fraction and then as a decimal. For example, if our unit were vacant 36 days, then—

$$\frac{36}{365} = 9.86\%$$

If our rent was $1,000 per year, then the expense of our vacancy expressed as dollars would be-

$$9.86\% \times \$1,000 \text{ or } \$98.60$$

Remember that it is common practice to deduct 10% vacancy factor as an expense. Anything you can prove to a buyer that is less than 10% is money in your pocket. See why you don't lose money if you move someone in for a few days free rent?

APPENDIX C

Property Tax Evaluation

When the assessor appraises your property, he breaks tax dollar into 3 parts:

- ✓ (a) Land
- ✓ (b) Improved property (buildings and structures and
- ✓ (c) Personal property (furniture, carpets, etc.)

This tax can then be broken down into percentages of each. This is usually used to determine your basis and how much depreciation you can use.

The government does not permit the **land** to be depreciated because theoretically it doesn't wear out.

The **improved property** will wear out so you are permitted to defray the cost of that building over a period of time. (The shorter the time, the higher the depreciation figure.) If the assessor determines that 70% of your property is improved property, then certainly the IRS will recognize that as being a fair figure. (You can set up a larger percentage, but you may be challenged by IRS to justify the basis).

The **personal property** would be those furnishings which are not part of the structure. Furniture, carpets, appliances, etc. These don't have the longevity of the structures, so they can receive an "excellerated" depreciation (depreciated in a much shorter span). The average estimated life for carpets in an apartment for instance, can be 5 years.

APPENDIX D

Effect of Income on the Value of Property

Capitalization Method

$$\text{Value} = \frac{\text{Net Income}}{\text{Capitalization Rate}}$$

An investor is going to expect a greater return on his money if the risk is higher. His return on income property is based on income. The more that is subtracted in expenses from that income, the less the value of the property. The better your property looks on paper, the better price it should bring.

The **capitalization rate** is not a constant figure. It is the rate of return an investor wants for a particular property. If the post office were to sign a lease for 20 years, there would be little risk, therefore a small return would be expected. If this same amount were invested in an older slum building that would require greater maintenance and vacancy, a higher rate would be expected.

Your city has different risk levels depending on area, age of buildings, vacancy and many other factors. This capitalization rate could vary from 5% (the post office) to 25% (our slum building). By closely studying the want ads you should be able to determine what the current rates are - certainly any knowledgeable realtor would know - give him a call. For this example, 8% will be used.

Step 1

gross income -- total revenue received from all means
less expenses -- management fees, utilities, taxes,
insurance services, repairs, paint, etc.

Net Income

The **Net Income divided by** the **capitalization rate** gives us the **Value** of the proprty.

Value = Net income ÷ Capitalization rate

If the New expenses are 5600 annually and we use a capitalization rate of 8%

$$.08\overline{)5600.00}\ = 70{,}000$$

The value of the property by capitalization would be 70,000.

Gross Multiplier Method

There is another way of approximating property value from the gross income called the "gross multiplier" (either monthly or annually). Since this figure doesn't take expenses into consideration, it gives you only a "ball park" figure.

With an annual gross multiplier of 8 and a gross income of $12000, then the value would be $96,000.

(8 x 12,000 = 96.000)

APPENDIX E

Depreciation

Definition: The amount ascribed to charging off the depreciating value of an aging property. This property could be a building, it could be improvements, it could even include producing plants, trees or vines.

Formerly an investor could start depreciation anew with each property when he acquired it.* IRS has changed this rule. Your depreciation now is carried from step to step when exchanged. Depreciation that has been written off is also subtracted from subsequent future properties as they are acquired.

A couple of terms come into focus at this time:

Recapture refers to IRS expectations of recapturing all or a portion of depreciation when property is sold. This recapture, depending on the type of depreciation used, will be either ordinary income or capital gain.

Cross-over point is the point in real estate investment were depreciation is no longer sufficient to render the property a tax loss.

*Therefore it is wise for the investor, **especially the estate builder,** to take out as little depreciation as possible or only as needed. This insures him more tax shelter down the road when he will need it more. This is also a clue as to why some of your early properties might be sold rather than exchanged. Somewhere in this process it might be to the investor's advantage to start anew with depreciation.

In intricate situations like these a knowledgeable realtor or tax advisor is worth the cost.

There are three basic methods of computing depreciation:
1. straight line method
2. declining balance method and,
3. sum of the digits method.

Straight line method - An equal amount is deducted each year until the entire value of the building is charged off. For tax purposes, this amount is charged off as an expense to the business. To find the depreciation, you divide the cost of the depreciable improvements by the economic life. What determines the economic life is somewhat debatable. The shorter the life, the greater the depreciation. The estate planner is not looking for tax shelter initially - he should try to guage this just sufficiently to avoid paying taxes on his property's income.

If we have a $100,00 building on a $33,000 lot, we can charge off that $100,000. If we elect a 40 year anticipated life for the building-

$$\frac{2,500}{40\,\overline{)100,000}}$$

we would charge $2,500 annually as an expense.

Declining balance method - Different types of new or used assets are depreciated at various rates such as 125%,

150%, or 200% of the original cost. This is known as an **accelerated method of depreciation.** For an estate builder this is not recommended. The more we charge off now, the less we will have to charge off later when we have more money involved.

These depreciation rates are really a variation of the straight line rate. If straight line rate is 2% (100,000 for 50 years), a 200% declining balance would be just double that - or 4%.

We would depreciate 100,000 4% the first year -

100,000 x .04 4,000
100,000 - 4,000 96,000

The second year we would depreciate -

96,000 x .04 3,840
96,000 - 3,840 92,160

The third year we would depreciate 92,160.

We would annually be depreciating from a **declining balance.**

Sum of the digits method - This is an accelerated method depreciation available only for new assets (not buildings). This is based on the expected life (or what the IRS will allow). We will depreciate something with an expected life of 5 years for example.

Add up the aggregate numbers from 1 to 5.

$$1 + 2 + 3 + 4 + 5 = 15$$

Now go backwards and take 5/15 of its value as depreciation the first year, 4/15's the second year, and so on until the last year when you take 1/15. If we were depreciating 10,000 worth of furniture the first year we could deduct

$$(5/15 = 1/3)$$
$$1/3 \times 10,000 = \$3,333.33$$

The second year we could deduct-

$$4/15 = 2.666$$
$$2.666\% \times 10,000 = 2666.70$$

The third year we could deduct-

$$3/15 = 1/5$$
$$1/5 \times 10,000 = 2,000.00$$

The fourth year-

$$2/15 = .1333$$
$$1.333\% \times 10,000 = 1333.33$$

The fifth year-
$$1/15 = 6.666\%$$
$$6.66 \times 10,000 = 666.67$$
$$\text{Total } 10,000$$

When **accelerated depreciation** is used, the IRS is expecting **recapture** as **ordinary income,** not capital gains.

$$10\% \quad .10 \times 100,000 \quad 10,000$$

(amount of depreciation to be taken on personal property)
If taken 5 years using sum of digits method

$$1 + 2 + 3 + 4 + 5 = 15$$

$$\frac{5}{15} \times 10,000 = 1/3 \times 10,000 = 3,333.33$$
(1st year depreciation)

2nd year not as much
$4/15 \times 10,000 = 2,666.67$

Straight line annual depreciation	2,000
Sum of Digits on personal property	+ 3,333.33
Total depreciation to be included as annual expense for tax purposes	(5,333.33)

For simplication on our example, we have disregarded the item on **interest.** It is a paper expense. In the early years of a Trust Deed almost all of the payment is going to interest. That portion going to principal (your equity) is negligible. To continue our over simplification, we are going to lean a little bit and say that all the payment is going to interest. Therefore all our payments are expense (but paper expense).

Income	Expense	cash expenses
12,000	4,000	interest
	+ 7,000	
12,000	- 11,000	= (1,000 cash flow)
	+ 5,333.33	
12,000		
-16,333.33	16,333.33	Total expenses for
		tax purposes
(4,333.33)	loss-tax shelter	

Sample Property

In order to give an example of many of these terms, we are going to buy a piece of property.

100,000 purchase price
 30,000 down payment
 12,000 gross annual income
  4,000 annual expenses (not including interest or depreciation)
  1,000 taxes (land 200, improvements 700, personal 100)
  7,000 total annual payments
    8% capitalization rate (8 gross multiplier)
    33 total days of vacancy

$$Value = \frac{Net\ Income}{Capitalization\ rate} = \$8,000$$

$$Value = \frac{Net\ income}{Capitalization\ rate} - \frac{\$,8,000}{.08} = \$100,000$$

(Value by Capitalization Method)

Value Gross multiplier x gross income

$$8 \times 12{,}000 = \$96{,}000$$

(Value by gross multiplier method)

Vacancy factor $\dfrac{33}{365} = .09$ or 9%

Vacancy factor expressed as dollar value

$$9\% = .09 \times \$12{,}000 = \$1{,}080$$

Gross Income minus (-) cash expenses - payments = cash flow

$$12{,}000 - (4{,}000 - 7{,}000) = 1{,}000$$

Property tax breakdown
  Taxes 1,000
  Improvements 700

$$1{,}000 \overline{)700.00}^{\;.70} = 70\%$$

$$1{,}000 \overline{)700.00}^{\;.10} = 10\%$$
Personal property
70% . 70 x 100,000 70,000
(amount of depreciation to be taken
on building)

Straight Line Method 35 years
70,000 35 = $2,000 per year depreciation on building

APPENDIX G

Sequence of Foreclosure

1. **Delinquency** - there is nothing to say how delinquent an account might be before foreclosure proceedings can be started. Actually, agreements are written into some contracts whereby the trust deed holder considers the owner delinquent if he doesn't keep the property up to standard. Most trust deed holders will wait until 2½ - 4 months before filing.

2. **Notice of default** - This shows the intent of the trust deed holder. It gives the occupant a period of 90 days to catch the account up to date. If the occupant has a sizeable equity in the property, he is motivated to sell and lots of people know it. The owner can also borrow money to pay the delinquent amount (and sometimes borrow more). For this amount, the owner can sign a note promising to pay a given amount at monthly intervals - the new lender then records this as a new trust deed. Because the former existing trust deed holds priority over this, the new trust deed is called a junior lien. There can be as many junior trust deeds as there are people who will lend money. Toward the end of the 90 day period the delinquent is progressively more motivated to sell, because the situation becomes more acute after that 90th day.

3. **Twenty-one day notice** - After the 90 day period has elapsed, the debtor is obliged to pay off the entire outstanding amount owed (plus penalties). This means that

he must find someone to refinance the whole amount or that he must sell out without 21 days.

A popular approach by speculators is to have the delinquent sign off all rights to his property. This can be done through the vehicle of a **quit claim deed.** In order to get him to do this, you offer the delinquent cash for his signature. It is then up to you to satisfy the trust deed holder. (In this 21 day period, the trust deed holder is apt to let the account come back to current status.) Perhaps you can talk him into rescinding the whole foreclosure. If not, then you will have to pay the entire balance.

4. If the trust deed holder stands firm for the entire amount owing, he will set up a date and place for a **Trustee Sale.** By law, this must be advertised weekly in a paper of major circulation for a period of 3 weeks preceding the sale. (Obviously, this is started 3 weeks prior to the end of the 90 day period). Sometimes the auctions are held within the lending institution, sometimes on the steps of the county courthouse. The auction is begun at the figure owed the party calling for the sale and the action proceeds from that figure.

APPENDIX H

Sample Properties

Here are some examples of actual properties, sales and transactions that took place in Southern California within a four week period in July and August, 1978. Opportunities like this are always available--it only takes a little diligence and digging on your part to seek them out.

Sample Property #1

July 3, 1978

A four bedroom house in Southeast San Diego was probably worth $45,000 with an existing $28,000 balance on the First Trust Deed.

The Second Trust Deed was being foreclosed upon at $3,500. There was only one qualified (with cash or cashier's checks) bidder who bid $1 over the Trust Deed original bid.

$$
\begin{array}{r}
\$28,000 \\
+\ \ 3,500 \\
\hline
\$31,500
\end{array}
$$

$$
\begin{array}{r}
\$45,000 \\
-\ \ 31,500 \\
\$14,500
\end{array}
$$

$14,500 ÷ $3,501 = 400% profit

July 25, 1978

The San Diego County Administrator held an auction of five properties. Several sold under the appraised value. Here are two illustrations:

Sample Property #2

One Vista property was appraised at $47,800 and was sold at $45,000. My feeling is that with only a little gardening and a little cosmetizing, this home would be worth about $52,000. This is right next to freeways and shopping centers in a very popular area. It could sell or rent easily.

Sample Property #3

A Rancho Bernardo home was appraised at $70,000, which is a low appraisal. This was auctioned at $70,500. Needing only some minor gardening and painting, this residence would easily bring $80,000 on the market. Rancho Bernardo is extremely popular, and there are few properties that bring less than $79,000--and those are smaller and with fewer bathrooms.

July 24, 1978

Under the flagpole at the La Jolla Post Office, two La Jolla glamour properties were auctioned under two different trustee sales (same trustor and trustee).

Sample Property #4

This house was appraised at $125,000. The total Trust Deed outstanding balances totaled $88,000. The $25,000 Second Trust Deed being foreclosed upon was purchased at $36,000. This home needed painting, carpeting and drapes. If we assume $10,000 for upgrading and back taxes:

$10,000 & $36,000 = $46,000 cash investment
$125,000 - $88,000 = $37,000 equity
$37,000 ÷ $46,000 = 80% profit

Sample Property #5

The other property was a large glamour executive home for entertaining with a fantastic view of La Jolla Shore. It was surrounded by homes valued at hundreds of thousands of dollars.

It was the consensus of many that the property was worth $200,000. (In fact, it was in escrow at the time for $197,000.) It finally sold for what really totaled $188,000. Somehow, this represents 6% under the market! Although this auction was spectacular (about 50 present with about 7 bidders) and still bought at a dollar price bargain, percentagewise it would not have been as good an investment as some others.

Sample Property #6

August 3, 1978

In December, 1976, a man paid $125,000 for a 2,000 + square foot contemporary home on a site with a view in San Diego County. The property was on a slight hill covering 2½ acres, completely enclosed with cyclone fence, horse corrals and about ½ acre in fruit trees. This is a prestigious neighborhood, with valuable horse ranches and classic old home.

Twenty months later at a trustee sale, this property was sold for:

$96,000	on the 1st TD
$25,000	on the 2nd TD
$ 2,000	on delinquent taxes
$123,000	

Property in San Diego County in 1977 on the average appreciated 33%. In the choice areas (such as this), the average was more. This property was easily worth:

$175,000	
-123,000	
$52,000	equity

The Second Trust Deed was foreclosed upon, and the penalties and costs brought the opening bid to approximately $34,000 and eventually sold for $35,000.

$52,000 ÷ 35,000 = 148.5% (if sold at $175,000)

Sample Property #7

August 9, 1978

A representative of the government (FNMA) held a trustee sale and no qualified bidders showed up. The property went back to the government for $44,670. Although run down, this place, with cosmetizing, would be a classy property with Pt. Loma, Coronado and San Diego Harbor view. It is in an area of mixed cultures.

It should be worth over $50,000--no real investment bargain. It will be completely refurbished by the government and sold as an FHA foreclosure and picked up for very little down--that could be a good investment if one would live there for a while and later sell it.

Sample Proprty #8

August 11, 1978

There was a sheriff's sale of 160 acres near Palomar Observatory. Eighty acres had been purchased for $80,000 and the other eighty for only about $12,000. This property, difficult to appraise, had to be worth $125,000.

Against this man was a judgment for $10,252 plus about $410 in expenses. This property was bid on at the judgment price and penalty only--there were no other bidders--not even any other observers:

$$\$125,000 \div \$10,660 = 1,172\% \text{ profit}$$

Summary of Sample Properties

After working TRUSTEE sales, PROBATE sales and SHERIFF sales full time for only a total of three weeks, it is obvious that there are bargains out there. Although one can spend vast amounts of time researching these properties, the bargains are there--and some outright steals. The higher cost properties aren't necessarily the best bargains. The better bargains seem to be away from the metro areas, with the exception of the submarginal areas. As previously suggested, suburban property listed by legal description only and posted only in the sheriff's office are often completely overlooked.

NOTES

I MADE OVER
ONE MILLION DOLLARS
($1,000,000)

Jim Stephenson, the former door to door vacuum cleaner sales-
man who turned $500.00 borrowed money into a million dollars
in less than five years.

YOU CAN TOO WITH THIS
SIMPLE MONEY MAKING SYSTEM!
WE WILL SHOW YOU HOW.

- To locate these properties.

- To finance these properties with
  as little as one hundred dollars
  down.

- To operate in your home, without
  a real estate license, and in your
  spare time.

- To resell these properties within
  thirty to sixty days with an extremely handsome profit.

YOU CAN

- Buy real estate far below the
  market value.

- Put money in the bank everytime
  you buy.

**Don't Delay — place your order in the mail today. Mail
$9.95 check, cash or money order payable to George Sterne
Agency, 8361 Vickers, Suite 304, San Diego, Ca. 92111.**

• BONUS •

If you order immediately I will send you a special edition of my system,
containing valuable material on how to borrow $500 to $5000 on just your
signature.

*Examine my system and special bonus for thirty days. If for any reason you
are not satisfied send back the material and your $9.95 will be promptly
refunded.*